IMAGES
of America

MAHANOY
AREA

IMAGES
of America

MAHANOY
AREA

Mahanoy Area Historical Society

ARCADIA
PUBLISHING

Published by Arcadia Publishing
Charleston, South Carolina

Library of Congress Catalog Card Number: 2004107308

For all general information, contact Arcadia Publishing:
Telephone 843-853-2070
Fax 843-853-0044
E-mail sales@arcadiapublishing.com
For customer service and orders:
Toll-Free 1-888-313-2665

Visit us on the Internet at www.arcadiapublishing.com

CONTENTS

ACKNOWLEDGMENTS

The production of this book would not have been possible without the unstinting cooperation of all those who provided the priceless images that lend incomparable depth and richness to this historical cavalcade. Photographic reproductions in this book come from the extensive archives of the Mahanoy Area Historical Society, as well as from the individual resources of various members.

For every pictorial contribution, the Mahanoy Area Historical Society extends the deepest and sincerest gratitude. Especially gratifying has been the generosity of those who made their family albums and other collections available. Your contributions will live on to enrich succeeding generations with a glimpse of the area that was home to their ancestors.

Deserving special acknowledgment in this regard are the Mahanoy Are Historical Society, the Mahanoy City Public Library, Vikki Ball, Michael Cheslock and Gary Senavites, Marie Ward Davidson, Christine Domson, Ray Eichman, Peg Grigalonis, Joan Goodman, Krista Gromalski, Howard "Bud" Holman, John Murtin, Bill O'Brien, Francis Senglar, and Frank Selgrath.

INTRODUCTION

This pictorial tour of the rugged slice of Appalachia called Mahanoy, nestled in the bosom of the northeast Pennsylvania anthracite fields, is a time-capsule journey from 1790 to 1913. The rich and vibrant history here played an integral part in the development and vitality of this great state and nation.

The word Mahanoy is from the language of the Native American tribes who frequented the area to hunt and fish. Land sale deeds that white settlers negotiated with Native Americans during the mid-1700s list the territory as "Maghonioy." The word translates to "salt lick," which refers to saline mineral deposits that attracted deer.

The geographic tract involved in this volume covers a contiguous cluster of six political subdivisions that make up the Mahanoy Area School District of northern Schuylkill County: the boroughs of Mahanoy City and Gilberton and the townships of Delano, Mahanoy, Rush, and Ryan.

The geologic terrain involved is highlighted by the convergence of two substantial mountains, the Mahanoy (also known as Broad Mountain) and the North Mahanoy (also known as Locust Mountain). This convergence creates three distinct valleys: the Mahanoy Valley, which carries the Mahanoy Creek westward for 50 miles to the Susquehanna River; the Quakake Valley, which carries the Quakake Creek eastward for 2 miles to the Little Schuylkill River; and the Locust Valley, which carries the Locust Creek eastward for 2 miles to the Little Schuylkill River.

The Mahanoy Valley is historic as a major coal-producing region. Quakake Valley is primarily agricultural. Locust Valley is noted for its agriculture, in addition to being the location of two major recreational tracts, the Locust Lake State Park and the Tuscarora State Park, located about five miles apart and fed mainly by Locust Creek.

The primary emphasis herein rests upon anthracite, since it was coal that brought birth and boom to the locality. This pictorial layout embraces the gamut of human experience in an era of drudgery, toil, hardship, and sacrifice, during which a few accumulated wealth while the many lived and died in the dreary throes of workaday anonymity. Yet, through it all, the spirit of the miners and their families shines through to paint the picture of a people who epitomized the tenacity and indomitable will of this rare breed of Americans.

It was the Civil War more than any other factor that brought the initial great thrust of activity to the Mahanoy coal field. The need for anthracite to fuel the war effort set off an influx of prospectors seeking the stores of coal buried beneath the terrain. By the time the war ended, the region was buzzing with mining operations.

Even greater demand for anthracite was created by the two world wars, which involved the United States. Also important to the industry was the use of coal to fuel the industrial revolution.

The reign of anthracite as the king of coal endured for almost a century until the industry collapsed in the mid-1950s, when oil, gas, and electricity began in earnest to replace coal as the nation's major sources of energy. Collapse of the mining industry left thousands of miners jobless and sank the entire northeast region of Pennsylvania into a state of depression, both economic and human. Today, the production of anthracite takes place on a vastly limited scale, compared with its glorious past.

Amid the throngs of ordinary people, the Mahanoy area has been home to its share of rich and famous. A few examples:

–As a boy, Pres. Franklin Delano Roosevelt rode the train from New York to spend summertime visits at a manorlike residence still standing and occupied in the Mahanoy Township village of New Boston. The residence was then owned by the Delano Land Company, a firm co-owned by the president's maternal grandfather, Warren Delano. Today, the township of Delano is named after Warren.

–Victor Schertzinger of Mahanoy City was a celebrated Hollywood director, composer, conductor, and producer during the first half of the 20th century.

–Lizzie (Stride) Arlington, world-famous female baseball player, was born at 438 West Centre Street in Mahanoy City in 1869. She played with the team from the First Ward, which included a one-armed pitcher, John Sabo, who was a wonder.

This overview should provide some idea of the historic cavalcade waiting in this presentation by the Mahanoy Area Historical Society.

—Mahanoy Area Historical Society Book Committee
Ray Eichman, Joan Goodman, Peg Grigalonis,
Krista Gromalski, Bill O'Brien, and Frank Selgrath

One

EARLY FAMILIES

Emanuel Boyer (inset) was Mahanoy City's first permanent resident. Boyer was born in 1829 in Schuylkill Township and moved to Mahanoy City with his family in 1853 as an agent for the Little Schuylkill Company. He built and operated the Mahanoy House Inn. Boyer remained in Mahanoy City until his death in 1913.

F. P. KLINE, Residence & General Store.

C. C. HAGENBUCH, Residence & Wholesale & Retail Drug Store. ESTABLISHED MAY 15TH 1862.

EXCELSIOR STEAM FLOUR MILLS.

METHODIST EPISCOPAL CHURCH & PARSONAGE. REV I.B. BROWN PASTOR

Residence of J. L. MATHIAS.

SMITH & BRO. General Store.

- 695231

PUBLIC SCHOOLS
HUMANE ENGINE HOUSE
QUEENS
BRICK HOUSE CHAS. R. KAIER
BAND CENTRAL HOTEL WM A. BENSINGER.
MANSION HOUSE JACOB BYERLY
MAHANOY VALLEY STATION
ELKHORN R.R. BREAKER
MAHANOY CITY GAS WORKS
EXCELSIOR IRON WORKS GEO. H. WREN. SUPT.
EXCELSIOR STEAM FLOUR MILLS.
WM COCKILL STEAM CARRIAGE WORKS.

MAHANOY
PENNSYLVANIA.
1889

DRAWN BY T. M. FOWLER, MORRISVILLE PA.

This is a picture of Mahanoy City in 1889, with a population of 6,892. The buildings above and below the map picture, from left to right, the following: (upper row) F. P. Kline's residence and general store, C. C. Hagenbuch's residence and wholesale and retail drugstore, Excelsior Steam Flour mills, A. & D. M. Hoppes Agents, Union National Bank, and the residence of John T. Quin; (lower row) the Methodist Episcopal church and parsonage, the residence of J. L. Mathias, Smith & Brothers general store, Reynolds & Company drugstore, Odd Fellows Hall, and the Kaier Opera House, which contained a post office, the Amphion Club, and a restaurant.

David Bowman (seated, far right) was a signer on the 1863 petition for the borough of Mahanoy City charter. He was part owner, with his brothers Peter and Jonas, in the firm that operated Bowman's Colliery and for whom Bowman's Patch was named. The family included company store managers, bankers, and colliery owners and was prominent in the early development of the town. Pictured in this 1898 photograph are Mr. and Mrs. David Bowman Sr., their three daughters, and their four sons, including David, a well-known photographer.

David Bowman Jr., an early resident of Mahanoy City, photographed prosperous families and major town events. One of his most popular subjects was his sister Pansy Bowman, seen here as a little girl with her two dolls.

Pansy Bowman is pictured as an aspiring photographer in the Bowman Studio, where both photographs shown on this page were taken. The studio was located at 19 West Mahanoy Avenue, the present site of the Mahanoy City Public Library.

This elegant photograph is of Pansy Bowman as a young woman in her finest new hat. Information about this and other work by David Bowman Jr. was obtained from *Reminiscences of Mahanoy City*, written by the photographer's granddaughter Augusta Dillman Thomas.

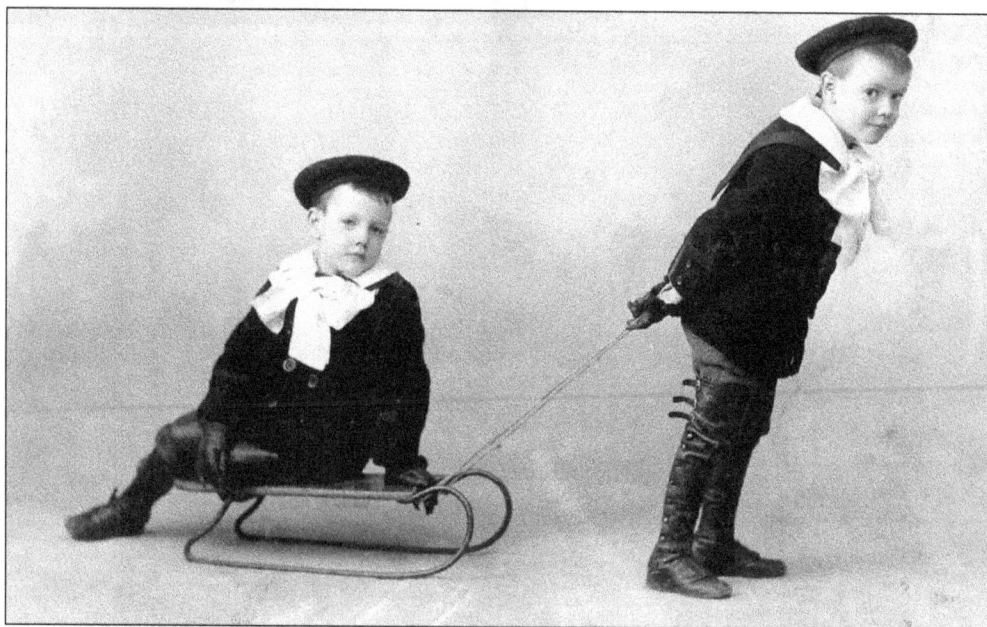

This wonderful portrait from the Bowman Studio captures mischievous boys in their Sunday best. At the time when David Bowman Jr. operated his Mahanoy City studio, there were no personal cameras and only wealthy individuals could afford portraits, most frequently made of their children. It was not until tintype became available in the 1880s that an inexpensive way to preserve memories became available to the working class.

Built in 1908 by John Smith at a cost of $40,000, this mansion on Mahanoy City's South Main Street looks much the same today as it did 100 years ago. It includes 14 rooms, 4 chandeliers, built-in wooden cabinets, and several stained-glass windows. The Smith family lived here until the 1970s. Currently, historical tours of the mansion are scheduled at Christmas and for special events throughout the year.

Pictured in the backyard of their mansion, facing west on Mahanoy City's South Main Street, are members of the John Smith family c. 1900. From left to right, they are as follows: (first row) Emmanuel, Vladimir, and Nicholas; (second row) Mary, John Sr., Anna, and John Jr.; (third row) Ella, Teckla, Augustine, Olga, and Anna. John Smith immigrated penniless to Mahanoy City in the 1880s and became a prominent banker and merchant. (Courtesy of Michael Cheslock and Gary Senavites.)

This Victorian Second Empire home was built in 1874 by Peter Otterbach, one of the first petitioners of the Mahanoy City charter. After his wife and young child died, Otterbach could no longer bear to live in the home where he had planned to spend many happy years with his family. He sold it to Matilda and Dr. Louis Weber. The Webers eventually sold the home to Margaret Curry Kaier, wife of Charles D. Kaier (founder of the Kaier Brewery), on May 11, 1891, and it became known as the Kaier Mansion. The mansion was sold 100 years later, in April 1991, at auction to Joan and James Goodman. Following a 13-month restoration, the Goodmans reopened the Kaier Mansion as a bed-and-breakfast. (Courtesy of Joan Goodman.)

16

Charles D. Kaier was born on March 6, 1839, in Biningan Baden, Germany. On January 8, 1863, he married Margaret Curry, a native of Schuylkill County, at St. Patrick's Church in Pottsville. Not only did he have the most complete and up-to-date brewery of his day, he also exercised an active interest in the Anthracite Light, Heat and Power Company, the Broad Mountain Water Company, and several other enterprises. Kaier was, at the time, the largest real-estate holder in Mahanoy City, and he gave the city one of the safest, prettiest, and best-equipped opera houses in northeastern Pennsylvania. (Courtesy of John B. Lieberman III.)

Margaret Curry Kaier, wife of Charles D. Kaier, had ten children; seven reached maturity, and three died at a very early age. After her husband's death on May 31, 1899, she became president of the Kaier Company, and her son Charles F. Kaier became secretary-treasurer. She died in December 1913, but there was much litigation involved with her will. By the time the estate was settled, World War I had begun and Prohibition had unsettled the family fortune. (Courtesy of John B. Lieberman III.)

Mary C. Kaier, known as Mame, operated the family brewery and opera house along with her brother Charles Kaier after their mother's death in 1913. She successfully petitioned the Philadelphia courts in 1918 to remove her brother as coexecutor of the Kaier estate because of his extravagant lifestyle. (Courtesy of John B. Lieberman III.)

Lloyd Fahler, a local photographer, pursued and later married Mame Kaier. Fahler was president of the Pennsylvania National Bank and eventually became president of the Kaier Brewery. (Courtesy of John B. Lieberman III.)

Here are "Champagne Charlie" Kaier and his friends at a picnic. From left to right are Johnny Williams, a Mahanoy City café proprietor; Kaier; Charlie Silliman, son of E. S. Silliman Sr. who founded the Silliman Colliery and Mahanoy City Water Company; and Reddy Haldeman, Mahanoy City's first auto mechanic.

This group of citizens on a tour of the Maple Hill Colliery mine shaft includes John B. Lieberman II (far right), who later became president of the Kaier Brewery. (Courtesy of John B. Lieberman III.)

Dr. David Holland (left), shown dissecting a cadaver, graduated from Medico-Chirurgical College (medical school) in 1903. He and his son, Dr. Mark Holland, cumulatively served the community of Mahanoy City as physicians from 1903 until the son's death in 1994. (Courtesy of the Holland family.)

Mark Holland was a pediatrician. Born in 1908, he is seen here as a child with his mother and father, Ella Cleary Holland and Dr. David Holland. (Courtesy of the Holland family.)

Mark Holland poses in his soldier costume. The same impish smile and playful spirit remained with him throughout his years as a pediatrician for the communities of Northern Schuylkill County. (Courtesy of the Holland family.)

In the early days of Mahanoy City, disease could spread rapidly if not properly treated. Measles, croup, scarlet fever, whooping cough, and diphtheria were prevalent, especially during the winter months. By the time Dr. David Holland began his practice in 1903, vaccinations were mandatory. Smallpox and influenza, for which there was no vaccination, killed many people, including the doctors who took care of the ill. (Courtesy of the Holland family.)

21

Grand Army Day, at one time observed every Labor Day in Mahanoy City, paid tribute to the valor and steadfastness of Civil War survivors of the Union army. Pictured here is Severn Post No. 110 Grand Army of the Republic, Mahanoy City Chapter, organized in 1868. With an original membership of 139, these 13 gathered on September 5, 1892, to uphold the charter of the Mahanoy City Chapter, which states, "before the people the lesson of the great struggle." The last member, Dallas Van Horn, survived until the late 1930s.

The Soldiers Monument is located in the German Protestant Cemetery in Mahanoy City. Completed in 1892, it was erected to honor the Civil War veterans. Frank F. Reed of Mahanoy City posed for the sculpture holding an actual bugle.

This early model six-shooter belonged to John Eichman, the first chief burgess of Mahanoy City. Born in Bavaria in 1817, Eichman immigrated to the United States with his wife and son in 1847. The family first settled in St. Clair and then moved to Mahanoy City in 1863. Eichman was a signer of the Mahanoy City charter. In 1864, he was elected the first executive of the newly created borough and was reelected to that position six more times. Eichman later served for many years as borough treasurer. He died in 1892 and is buried in St. Fidelis Cemetery.

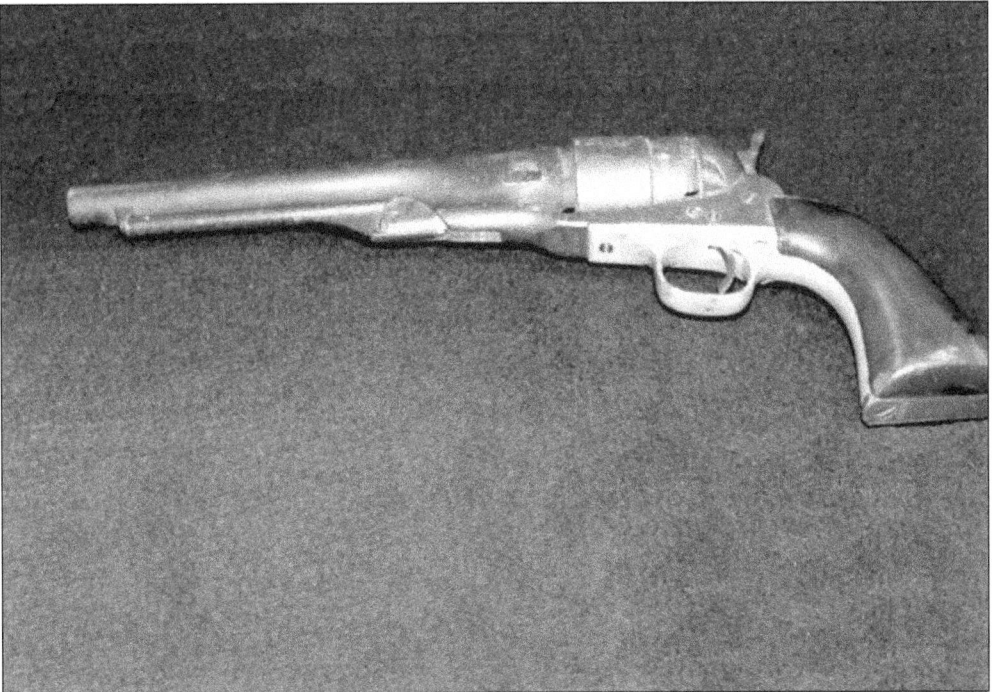

Leon Eckert came to Mahanoy City from Germany in the 1880s. His wife, Marguerite Huebner, was also from Germany. Almost immediately after coming to the city, Eckert opened a butcher shop at 301 West Pine Street that he operated until his retirement in the 1920s. In addition to his business, Eckert was a leader in banking, church, and civic affairs. (Courtesy of David Huebner.)

Original owners Leon and Marguerite Eckert are pictured in their butcher shop, built in the late 1800s at 301 West Pine Street in Mahanoy City. Eckert slaughtered his own meats, made sausages and puddings, and operated a grocery store. The original cash register and the tools used to slaughter the animals are still preserved by Eckert's great nephew, David Huebner. (Courtesy of David Huebner.)

Edward Hawkes is dressed as a soldier outside of his home, at 1117 Water Street in Mahanoy City. He was the nephew of David Hawkes, the adopted son of Leon Eckert who became the proprietor of the Eckert butcher shop after his father's death. This picture was taken on the day of a town parade. (Courtesy of Peg Grigalonis.)

While the men were at work in anthracite coal mines, wives and children went to culm banks to pick coal for heating their homes and cooking their meals. Mothers had to take their toddlers along, since the children were too young to be home alone.

Posing for this 1904 photograph are the four oldest children of Giuseppe and Maria Louisa Fanelli. Their parents emigrated from Italy and raised their children in a mom-and-pop tailor shop on East Mahanoy Avenue in Mahanoy City. Pictured from left to right, the boys are Johnny, Danny, Bill, and Albert. (Courtesy of Marjorie Fletcher.)

Two

DOWNTOWN

The Kaier Grand Opera House, located on the corner of Main and Market Streets in Mahanoy City, opened in 1896. The building contained the theater, A. J. Kelly's Café, a stockroom, a lumber room, a dining room, and a dance hall. It was the proud showplace of the region until it was destroyed by fire on October 15, 1913. Margaret Kaier announced a new and better theater would be built at the same location; she died two months later and her plans were not fulfilled. Instead, the lot was sold to Chamberlain Enterprises for construction of the Victoria Theatre in 1923.

Ladies' Dining Room Kaier Opera House, Mahanoy City, Pa.

The Kaier Opera House included the Ladies' Dining Room and the Kaier Opera House Bar. It existed for 28 years until its destruction by fire in 1913. For its first 8 years, it was known as the Kaier Opera House. After 3 years of renovations, it became known as the Kaier Grand Opera House, and it was known as that for its remaining 17 years.

Kaier's Opera House Bar, Mahanoy City, Pa.

This horse-drawn wagon transporting Kaier beer barrels along Mahanoy City's North Main Street was once a familiar scene in town. The Hotel Kaier (left), at 41-43 North Main Street, was demolished to make way for expansion of Charles D. Kaier's brewery facilities.

This postcard pictures the dining room in the Kaier Hotel, located at 41-43 North Main Street, in 1896. Because travel between towns was usually an overnight voyage on horse, there were 27 hotels in operation in Mahanoy City at this time.

The Union Cooperative Building, pictured c. 1860, was a center of commerce on the northwest corner of Main and Centre Streets in Mahanoy City. Its wood awning extended out over the sidewalk, providing a perch that was a good vantage point from which to watch parades and activities in the town. The Union Cooperative Building was replaced in 1922 by the Union National Bank. Later occupants were Woolworth's store and Dollar General. Currently, the building houses offices for the Area Revitalization and Development Corporation and the Mahanoy Area Historical Society.

Pictured is Mahanoy City's justice of the peace office in the Union Cooperative Building. From left to right are Robert Geiger, coal and iron police officer; Honorable Alexander May, justice; ? Marsh, janitor of the Spruce Street School; Reverend Lohr, pastor of St. John's Lutheran Church. May was a justice of the peace for 25 years. He was also a local realtor and insurance agent.

30

Labor Day, once known as Grand Army Day, brought decorators from Williamsport, Norristown, Allentown, Reading, and Philadelphia to trim houses and businesses with flags and bunting. Beautiful arches were erected at Main and Centre Streets, Catawissa and Centre Streets, Mahanoy and Main Streets, Fourth and Centre Streets, and Eighth and Centre Streets. Photographer David Bowman captured many photographs of the festivities, including this one. Information given here was adapted from *Reminiscences of Mahanoy City*, by August Dillman Thomas, a Bowman descendent.

The Nicholas Huber Furniture store was located at 109 East Centre Street in Mahanoy City. Along with selling furniture, Huber Furniture advertised "undertaking was a specialty" in the town's 50th-anniversary booklet. It was common practice at the time for merchants to sell coffins and provide horse-drawn buggies for burials.

Union National Bank,
Mahanoy City, Pa.

This magnificent brownstone, still located at the corner of Centre and Locust Streets in Mahanoy City, was originally built by the Union National Bank in 1889. The first bank at this location was the Citizen's Bank, formed in 1868 by David Bowman, which failed in 1873 amidst a financial depression. The Union National Bank flourished and, by 1920, needed larger quarters. The old Union Cooperative Building, at 1 West Centre Street, which had served the community since its beginning, was torn down, and the new Union National Bank opened in 1922. Its final move was in 1937, when the Union National Bank assumed all liabilities of the First National Bank, located at 1 East Centre Street. Presidents of the Union National Bank were Andrew Comer, Harrison Ball, Wilbur Barlow, Joseph Ferguson, Lloyd W. Fahler, and Russell Forster.

This postcard shows the Union National Bank decorated for a town celebration. "Interest paid on savings accounts" is written on the bank window.

The First National Bank was incorporated in 1864 in a rented brick storeroom on the northeast corner of Main and Centre Streets. It was the first national bank in Schuylkill County. The granite building (above) was built while the bank continued to serve the citizens of the Mahanoy Valley. In 1937, because of increasing liabilities, it was taken over by the Union National Bank. First National Bank presidents were Abraham Focht, Nicholas Balliet, Edward S. Silliman Sr., Edward S. Silliman Jr., and Fred Beck.

Built in 1863 by the Little Schuylkill Company, the Mansion Hotel was Mahanoy City's premier hotel. Of brick and stucco construction, it was four stories high in front, with an exterior porch on the second floor facing Centre Street. Because travel was so much more laborious in the 19th century, hotels were a thriving business in every town. Many important citizens visited Mahanoy City, including gubernatorial candidates and theater stars. All of them stayed at the Mansion.

In the early 1900s, the Hersker Theater was located at the site of today's Uni-Mart. Lettering on the face of the building identifies it as Hersker's Theater, but the marquee indicated that it was then operated under the name of Family Theater. At five stories, it was the tallest building on Mahanoy City's main thoroughfare, and its unique architecture made it stand out in the crowd.

A huge eagle atop 9 East Centre Street identified the home of the Mahanoy City Fraternal Order of Eagles Aerie No. 167 in the early 1900s. The building is pictured at its dedication in April 1907. It remained intact until gutted by fire in March 1946. Currently, the site is occupied by the Nelson Davis Insurance Agency.

John Mitchell, president of the United Mine Workers of America, was so beloved that mineworkers declared October 29 a holiday called Mitchell Day. It was celebrated annually in Mahanoy City, as seen here.

Looking east, this early postcard view is of Centre Street in Mahanoy City. Note the poles for electricity and telephone service, erected shortly after 1888. The streets are still unpaved, but wooden awnings have been constructed in front of businesses to protect shoppers. Because hot water in homes was rare, most residents bathed only once a week. These boys in short pants (knickers) and the girls in light dresses and cotton stockings are attired most likely in their Sunday best after their Saturday night bath. Moustaches, some long and shaped like bicycle handlebars, are seen on the men at the right.

This early-1900s photograph shows Chas Lieberman's tavern, on North Main Street in Mahanoy City. The Kaier Brewery is in the background. (Courtesy of Joan Goodman.)

This photograph of North Main Street shows the wood-sided homes, the cobblestone street with cable-car rails, Chas Lieberman's tavern, and the Kaier Brewery in the background. (Courtesy of Joan Goodman.)

H. J. Heiser Company, the interior of which is seen here, was a store that sold everything. In 1854, Edward F. Smith opened a hardware and tinsmith business and eventually sold it to George Seligman (left) and Harry J. Heiser (center). In 1885, the partnership was dissolved and Heiser became the sole proprietor. After Heiser's death, his son-in-law William F. Peters continued the business. After Peters's death, longtime employee Frank Pangonis continued to operate the store for Peters's widow, the former Marion Heiser. Upon the death of Marion Heiser Peters, Frank Pangonis acquired full interest in the store. As of 2004, after 53 years, Pangonis is still happily serving the public. (Courtesy of the Pangonis family.)

Nathan Bohorad is pictured with his wife, Bessie Posner Bohorad, and three of their six children, from left to right, Sarah, Sam, and Harry. Their three younger children were Esther, James P., and Herman. The parents were born in Russia and immigrated to Mahanoy City, where Bohorad opened a men's clothing store at the southwest corner of Centre and Linden Streets, a site currently occupied by McLaren's Auto Supply. The family lived behind and above the store, kept a cow in the backyard for milk and beef, and kept chickens for eggs. Bohorad later moved the clothing store to 34 West Centre Street, where he was joined by his sons Harry and Herman, who succeeded him as owner. (Courtesy of Robert Bohorad, Esq.)

Richard H. Guinan built this large wooden department store in the mid-1890s at 201–203 West Centre Street to sell furniture, appliances, and miscellaneous housewares to the quickly growing Mahanoy Valley communities. Guinan was helped by his mother, Catherine, brother Daniel, and wife, Julia. His department store thrived through the decades, until the devastating Memorial Day fire in 1941. When rebuilt, the new store was an all-brick structure with an extensive sprinkler system. This building is now the home of Service Electric Cable TV & Communications. (Courtesy of Peg Grigalonis.)

Young Catherine and Daniel Guinan are pictured in front of their family store. In the window can be seen a highchair and large picture framed in gold leaf. (Courtesy of Peg Grigalonis.)

Taken in 1912, this photograph is of Julia Whalen Guinan, her infant son Daniel, and Catherine, her eldest. Julia Whalen was one of seven students to graduate from Coles High School in 1903. She taught school for several years before marrying Richard H. Guinan and helping him run his department store, begun in 1897. (Courtesy of Peg Grigalonis.)

Banking was an important part of the growth of Mahanoy City. In 1903, the Merchants Bank, originally located at the southeast corner Main and Center Streets, was founded by David Graham and Daniel F. Guinan. In the 1920s, the imposing structure pictured here was built for the growing bank. The Merchants Bank was consolidated with the American Bank in 1930, and the building stood unused until the early 1950s, when it became the borough's Teen Canteen. Today, it serves the community as the Mahanoy City Recreation Center. (Courtesy of Peg Grigalonis.)

Many immigrants operated storefront businesses in their homes while raising their families. Maria Louise Fanelli (left) peeks out of the Fanelli Tailor Shop, where she did alterations, while Merle and Ruth Wesner pose outside their parents' grocery store (right). (Courtesy of Marjorie Fletcher.)

Bill Fanelli, son of Giuseppe Fanelli, stands in front of the family tailor shop. The sign on the right reads "Ladies tailoring and cleaning." (Courtesy of Marjorie Fletcher.)

Leopold and Florence Fanelli sit in front of the Wesner Grocery Store, in the 700 block of Mahanoy Avenue in Mahanoy City. Note the political posters and goods for sale in the window. (Courtesy of Marjorie Fletcher.)

One-year-old Leopold Fanelli is seen in the backyard of his home, at 729 East Mahanoy Avenue in Mahanoy City, in the early 1900s. Although homes were only 12.5 feet wide, they each had a small backyard planted with grass and flowers. (Courtesy of Marjorie Fletcher.)

In the early days of the Mahanoy area, farmers lived in the surrounding valleys and miners lived in surrounding company towns or patches. There were no cars or paved streets, so it was common for housewives to have things delivered to their homes. Leon Eckert, a butcher, and his horse and cart are on his weekly route, offering fresh meats and dry goods to customers. (Courtesy of David Huebner.)

Along with lumberjacks and carpenters, some of the first businessmen in Mahanoy City were undertakers. This photograph of Eddie Haughney, taken on West Market Street, shows him sitting on the Haughney funeral hearse. The hearse was used in the 1890s to take the coffin of the deceased to church and to the cemeteries located up the steep "Pottsy hill," nicknamed because it leads to Pottsville. (Courtesy of Haughney family.)

William Truskowski (original spelling) sits atop the family hearse in 1905 with the funeral entourage in front of St. Mary's Byzantine Catholic Church, located in the 600 block of West Pine Street in Mahanoy City. (Courtesy of Louis Truskowsky.)

Dr. David Holland makes his rounds of patients throughout the Mahanoy area. Horses and wagons were kept in stables on Railroad and Maple Streets and used daily by businessmen and professionals. (Courtesy of the Holland family.)

The Thomas and Elizabeth Orr Goodwin family is pictured, from left to right, as follows: (first row) Alexander, Elizabeth, Elizabeth Orr, and Robert; (second row) Ruth Doc, Jeannette, Thomas, Margaret, Ann, and Janet. Elizabeth Orr was a matriarch who emigrated from Scotland. Family members have served on the local school board, as mayor, and as operators of an icehouse and café. Direct descendants of the Goodwin family still operate the West End Café. (Courtesy of Lois Morgan.)

McCann's School of Business, founded in Mahanoy City in 1897 by L. C. McCann, continues to provide quality education in business and technology. It was originally housed on North Main Street in the Thompson Building, as pictured, but the school has also been located on the second floor of the present Mahanoy City Visitor's Center and in the D Street School Building and is currently on South Main Street.

This is a picture of Thomas Tregellas in the late 1800s, proprietor of the Tregellas Shoe store, originally located at 34 East Centre Street in Mahanoy City. Tregellas later moved his store across the street to 33–35 East Centre Street, which is now Carini's restaurant. On September 22, 1963, when the community observed its centennial, Tregellas, at 97 years old, was the oldest active businessman, having established his business 77 years before. He was the oldest living graduate of the Mahanoy City High School, being a member of the class of 1884.

Beginning at the corner of Centre and Locust Streets, the *Mahanoy City Directory* (1899) lists the businesses in the first block of West Centre Street. On the south side, beginning on the right, are the following: No. 38, Union National Bank; No. 36, merchant and tailor Philip Coffee; No. 34, book binder Michael Moore and lawyer Joseph Brown; No. 32, lawyer I. Y. Sollenberger; No. 30, hats and gents furnishings retailer John Fred Bernet; No. 28, boot and shoe salesman George Post; No. 24, baker and confectioner Louis Karkompasis (later known as George's); No. 22, druggist Myers (later known as Timm's Pharmacy); No. 20, boot and shoe salesman Thomas Patterson; No. 18, Smith Seager's variety store; No. 12 watchmaker and jeweler Ben J. Franklin; and on the corner of Centre and South Main Streets, the Mansion House Hotel.

Centre Street, looking West — Mahanoy City, Pa.

This early postcard of the business district in 1899 depicts the scene across Centre Street from the view in the previous photograph. Beginning at the corner of Centre and Main Streets, the *Mahanoy City Directory* (1899) lists the businesses on the right as the Union Co-Op, butcher Thomas Quinn (rear), Penn Telephone, the Grand Central Hotel, Adams Express, the Fister Millinery, confectioner Cleary, George Dennis dry goods, milliner M. J. Carley, the Outlet (tailor), druggist Thomas Flanigan, Mrs. McGuire's Saloon, and druggist Thomas McGuire.

Three

CHURCHES AND SCHOOLS

Built by Scotch settlers in 1862, one year before the town was officially incorporated, the First Presbyterian Church was the first place of worship of any denomination in Mahanoy City. It remains on the southeast corner of Main and South Streets. The interior features the original tin walls and ceiling, which have been meticulously maintained by the parishioners. On June 23, 1862, the town's first Sunday school was established, with Kate Thompson, wife of Dr. Louis M. Thompson, serving as superintendent. (Courtesy of Michael Cheslock and Gary Senavites.)

PRESBYTERIAN CHURCH, SO. MAIN ST.
MAHANOY CITY, PENNA.

St. Canicus Church—Mahanoy City, Pa.

In 1863, Irish immigrants built the first Catholic church in Mahanoy City on Catawissa Street on the site of the present-day parking lot. The first pastor, Rev. Michael McAvoy, named the church after a holy Irish abbot and patron saint of his native town, St. Canicus of Kilkenny, Ireland. This edifice was used until 1924, when a combination church and school was built. From its beginning, St. Canicus was known as "the Irish church."

Lithuanian settlers built this impressive church in the late 1890s. St. Joseph's Church is a brick building featuring three front entrances, vaulted ceilings, and a choir loft. From its beginning to the present day, priests assigned to this parish have spoken Lithuanian and heard confessions in the language.

Built by German Catholics in 1866, St. Fidelis Church was a red brick building with windows of ordinary glass and no vestibule, tower, steeple, or bells. Pictured here, it looks as it did in the late 1800s, when the steeple, bells, and stained-glass windows were added. Still in use are the pews (1909), main altar (1914), and Stations of the Cross in German.

St. Fidelis School, the first parochial school in Mahanoy City, was established in 1868 by Rev. Francis Buening. With his brother as a teacher and organist, the Buenings conducted the school for six years until the sisters of St. Francis from Glen Riddle were sent to teach. The school progressed rapidly, necessitating the building of a second, larger school (pictured here). Of wooden frame, it had six classrooms, an auditorium, two kitchens, and a social hall for church functions and weddings. In 1961, the school was permanently closed.

Local families frequently had group photographs taken on their church steps and at the open casket funerals of their relatives. This picture, taken in front of St. Joseph's Lithuanian Church, shows the casket open at the top and on the side, and the clock set at the time of the beloved's death. (Courtesy of Bernard Marchalonis.)

This 1898 photograph shows St. John the Baptist group members gathered in front of their wooden church, the Assumption of the Blessed Virgin Mary. Shortly after arriving in Mahanoy City, a small group of Slovaks gathered to build this church, which was used until the current brick building was erected in 1928.

The difficult life of mining families can be seen on the somber faces of these children as they shovel snow from in front of the Assumption of the Blessed Virgin Mary rectory. The children are, from left to right, Sue and Agnes Hovence, Testen Zapac, Helen Lazor, Vera Bondrowski, Joe Hovenice, and J. Pollack.

The first Polish immigrants arrived in Mahanoy City in 1873, but a congregation was not established until 1894, when the old Welsh Baptist Church, on South Catawissa Street, was purchased. A second church was destroyed by fire, and the present St. Casimir's Church (pictured) was built in 1927, featuring two steeples, a circular stained-glass window, and wonderful acoustics.

According to the Christ Lutheran (Evangelical) Church's 50th anniversary booklet from 1914, a sermon was preached to a number of German people in the early part of 1863 in the existing Presbyterian church in Mahanoy City. By 1864, a church (pictured) was built, but a year later, "customs that were unlutheran caused a split," and, by agreement, the faction that paid the highest sum held the church. Bankruptcy, a sheriff sale, and a fire did not deter the sturdy Germans. By 1914, the church was valued at $40,000 and had 700 members. In 1937, the old church was razed and the present edifice, at the same location on Main and Mahanoy Streets, was built.

The original St. Paul's United Church of Christ, at South Main and Maple Streets, was sold in 1906 for use as a garment factory when property was purchased to build a new church at Main and Pine Streets. This church, pictured on an early postcard, is highlighted by wonderful stained-glass windows and vaulted ceilings. In 1948, fire damaged St. Paul's, but the building was soon remodeled and is an active parish today, known for its hand-bell choir.

This early postcard features the Sunday School Room of St. Paul's United Church of Christ, located on the first floor in the center of the main church room. Parish children from infancy to age 12 attend weekly lessons that prepare them for confirmation. The room is also used for Rally Day, when students move from the primary to the junior level and are awarded their own Bible. This room looks the same today as it does in this nearly-100-year-old picture.

The first local effort toward forming an evangelical society was in the years 1859 to 1860, when occasional meetings were held in Mahanoy City. The first church, Salem Evangelical, was built at Spruce and Catawissa Streets in 1866. It was later sold to the Holy Emmanuel Slovak Lutheran Church when the Evangelical congregation purchased the land for the church pictured here. Built in 1904, the Salem Evangelical Church still stands at the corner of Fourth and Centre Streets in Mahanoy City. A unique feature of the red brick building is the infant room entrance near the rear of the church, where children from birth are welcome to come and worship.

This is a picture of the Boys Brigade of the First Methodist Episcopal Church. Rev. Benjamin La Pish (right foreground) was the captain.

While their church was being built, parishioners of the First Methodist Episcopal Church worshiped in a tent on West Mahanoy Avenue. On April 21, 1865, the foundation of the church was begun, and, on July 1, the cornerstone was laid. The present edifice was completed on October 29, 1893, at a cost of $21,000.

This artist's rendition is of the original white church (1831–1884). Pioneer residents of Rush Township, in Schuylkill County, worshiped in the home of John Neifert from c. 1799 to 1809 and in a partially built log church from 1809 until 1831. The cornerstone of the original white Christ Church (pictured) was not laid until 1831. It was 30- by 35-feet in dimension and of log and weatherboard construction, with only two hymnals, one used by the preacher and the other by the organist. This structure was abandoned when the new white church was built in 1884.

In 1846, the Christ Evangelical Lutheran and Reformed Church was inaugurated and land in Barnesville, across the highway from the original white church and near the present-day Marian High School, was purchased from the grandson of John Neifert. The cornerstone for the new church was laid in 1884, and the structure was painted white in contrast to the green of the woods and fields. The United Church of Christ and the Lutheran congregation continue to worship in this church today.

According to the church's 150th anniversary booklet, St. Peter's Church in Locust Valley (pictured) was built in 1847 on land in Rush Township (now Ryan). The McKnight family donated the land to provide a "combined Lutheran and Reformed house of the Lord in equal rights of both congregations in the German and English languages." It was built by church members Levi Blew, John Schlier, and William Faust. The church was rebuilt and remodeled in 1899, and, in 1944, it was converted to a Colonial-style church, with a new heating system and electric lights that replaced kerosene ones. In 1989, an addition closed the outhouses and brought bathrooms indoors. Today, the church is still famous for its Strawberry Social, begun in the 1960s as a fund-raiser.

The Bethany United Methodist Church in Barnesville stands on land given by Jacob and Catherine Faust to the Evangelical Association to be used as a church and cemetery. The church was dedicated in November 1873. Eventually, the United Evangelical Church was formed from the Evangelical Association. In 1923, a major division took place, and the congregation voted to remain in the Evangelical denomination. The church merged with the United Brethren in Christ to form the Evangelical United Brethren Church in 1947. In 1968, the Evangelical United Brethren Church and the Methodist church joined to become the present Bethany United Methodist Church.

Charles D. Kaier—pioneer, resident, and brewing company owner—is buried with his family at the St. Fidelis German cemetery. This towering stone monument of the blessed mother lists on its front the following: Troian Anselm Kaier, born February 10, 1874, died February 11, 1874; Chas D. Kaier, born March 6, 1839, died May 31, 1899. The back of the monument lists the following: Annie Kaier, born November 11, 1871, died May 20, 1874; Mary Kaier Fahler, born May 11, 1875, died November 15, 1937. Each side of the monument lists the following: Lloyd W. Fahler, born February 4, 1866, died September 15, 1977; Chas F. Kaier, born September 17, 1879, died October 13, 1921; John B. Lieberman, born April 25, 1863, died March 24, 1907; Ella Kaier Lieberman, born January 16, 1865, died July 20, 1895; Margaret Kaier Lieberman, born June 5, 1870, died September 19, 1932; and Margaret Curry Kaier, born March 15, 1839, died December 4, 1913.

This is a picture of Peter Otterbach's grave and tombstone. Otterbach was one of the petitioners of Mahanoy City's charter. Many of the signatures on the original petition are difficult to decipher. For example, the name of Peter Otterbach is recorded as John Ellenbach. Otterbach was one of the first directors of the First National Bank and an owner of a hotel on the first block of East Centre Street. He built the most magnificent house, now known as the Kaier Mansion, for his wife and young child, both of whom died before it was completed.

No picture remains of the first school built in the borough of Mahanoy City, although it is described in the writings of Augusta Dillman Thomas as a log structure on Spruce Street near Linden Street, with a middle aisle, rows of desks and benches on each side. Each bench was occupied by a half dozen or "as many as could be crowded thereon at times." In 1863, the brick Spruce Street School (pictured) was erected, and additions were added in 1875 and 1907. Originally, it had four rooms and four teachers. Within two years, the Mahanoy City school district had between 600 and 700 names on their rolls. The schools at that time were graded as primary, grammar, secondary, and high.

In 1893, the Eighth Street School was erected because of the growing student population in the east end of Mahanoy City. The school was located at the northeast corner of the present Pine and 12th Streets. It was renamed the Twelfth Street School in 1914 because of the change in street names. Inside the Twelfth Street School were eight classes, a small health room, a toilet, and storage facilities. There was no library, gym, or cafeteria. The interior had beautiful wood trim and hardwood floors. Today, a private residence replaces the school on its large lot.

This is a picture of a fourth-grade class in front of the Twelfth Street School building in 1896. Augusta Dillman (center) was the teacher.

In 1871, the first Centre Street School, a three-story brick building, was erected at a cost of $20,000. Solomon Lutz was the contractor. The east room on the third floor was used as a high school until 1880, when the high school was moved to the old Pine Street building. Eventually, the old Centre Street School building was razed and a new two-story brick high school was built in 1916, with separate entrances for girls and boys, a regulation basketball court, and a pit, or below-ground-level practice court. The Centre Street building was demolished in the 1980s and today is the site of Herman's Community Park. (Courtesy of Michael Cheslock and Gary Senavites.)

This is a picture of children of the first primary grade with their teacher, Jeanette Hornsby, in front of the old Center Street School building in 1910.

This is a picture of a fourth-grade class in front of the Center Street Annex in 1916.

Pine St. School Building, Mahanoy City, Pa.

In 1867, four years after the first school was built on Spruce Street, a second school was needed because of the influx of many Welsh, Irish, English, and German immigrants coming to work in the coal mines. With Solomon Faust as the contractor, the Pine Street School was built at a cost of $7,600.

This is a picture of the children of the third primary grade in front of the Pine Street School building in 1896. Mary Moll was the teacher, and James Norris was the janitor.

Teacher Carrie Hassel (51) stands with her students at the Pine Street School. From left to right are the following: (first row) Walter Dennis (1), unidentified (2), Bill Harris (3), unidentified (4), Dilchues (5), Tony Rich (6), William Maberry (7), George Miller (8), Larry Brennan (9), and John Rausch (10); (second row) Emily Dilcher (11), Mary Kirchner (12), R. Dregai (13), Carrie Blew (14), Merel Wessner (15), Agnes Bendinsky (16), Anna Whalen (17), Larue Kemersal (18), Mae Thomas (19), and Marie Tempest (20); (third row) Evan Johns (21), unidentified (22), Harry Bohorad (23), Kathryn Kerkusky (24), Ethel Sohaffer (25), Blanch Barnhardt (26), Pearl Brispack (27), E. Schwient (28), Margaret Starky (29), Petronella Yarnosky (30), Martha Johns (31), Gailgnt ? (32), and Mary McElhenny (33); (fourth row) Charles Eckrow (34), Kershutsky (35), Sissy "Babe" Reese (36), unidentified (37), Dan Fanelli (38), Dan Rinkenberger (39), Dick Russell (40), and Harry Bartlet (41); (fifth row) unidentified (42), Catherine O'Connor (43), Bessie Eckert (44), Tillie Richards (45), and Kathryn Schatzline (46); (sixth row) Doloris Reardox (47), Ethel Reardon (48), Dolores Reardon (49), and Kathryn Broderick (50). (Courtesy of Marjorie Fletcher.)

High school teachers and their pupils pose in front of the Pine Street School building in 1889.

Pictured in the 1890s with their teacher, Sister Monica, are the students of St. Fidelis Sister School. The name "Sister School" came from the nuns who were the administrators and teachers of the school. Catherine Klitsch Hawkes (1886–1958) labeled this picture with the names of her brother and their friends as follows: John Martin (first row, third from the left); Carrie Krauts, Mary Keller's mother (second row, fifth from the left); Katie Grims (second row, seventh from the left); Mrs. Post, Rita's mother (second row, eleventh from the left); Mary Maser Hampton (third row, second from the left); Mame Keller Goodman (third row, ninth from the left); Sister Monica (third row, thirteenth from the left); and Henry Klitsch (fourth row). (Courtesy of Peg Grigalonis.)

This is an artist's rendition of the first school in Rush Township. The school is described as a log house, located a mile from the village of Barnesville, according to the history of Barnesville centennial booklet dated 1954. A table was in the center of the room, and the pupils sat around it on backless benches. Individual instruction was given in "the three R's: Reading, Ritin, and Rithmetic." John Faust, ancestor of longtime librarian Thelma Faust of the Mahanoy City Public Library, is credited with starting the first school in the township, although an exact date cannot be determined. It was many years before a "common school-state run school was petitioned for in 1853." Most of the early settlers in Rush Township were Germans, and the German language was the only one taught in school. A Prussian named Francis Keenly was the first instructor. Later, English teachers were employed, one of whom was Mary Blew, ancestor of Eleanor Blew, a well-known music teacher during the latter part of the 20th century.

Jane M. Lyon taught in the Mahanoy City schools from 1870 to 1879. The wife of Judge T. H. B. Lyon of the Schuylkill County Orphans Court, she wrote in 1905 *History of Mahanoy City and the Building of the Mahanoy Tunnel*, a work that is still regarded as one of the most authoritative on the early history of the borough.

This is a picture of the graduating class of 1885 in Mahanoy City.

This picture of the Mahanoy City graduating class of 1876 includes superintendent William L. Balentine (front left) and principal Godfrey Wade (front right).

Pictured are Mahanoy City graduates of bygone days. From left to right are Thomas Tregellas, class of 1884; Emily Tregellas, class of 1880; Jennie Morris, class of 1882; and Dr. Arthur Jones, class of 1876.

These three members of the first graduating class of 1875 are identified, from left to right, as Allen Swalm, Thomas J. Parmley, and Charles Snyder.

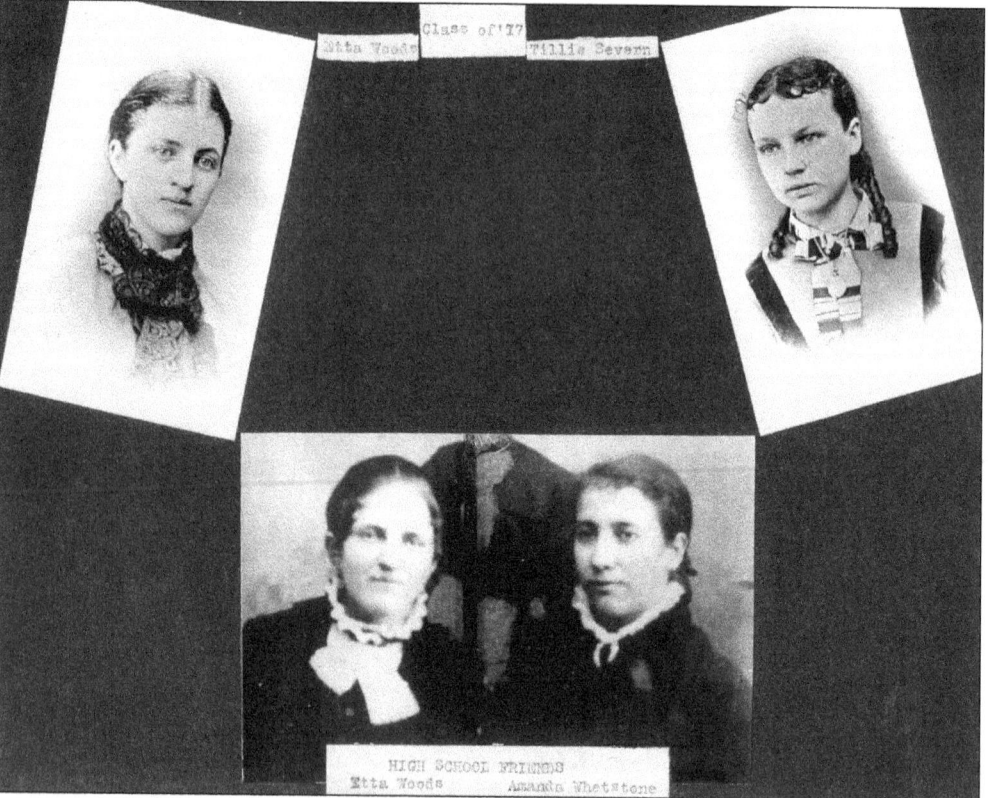

Pictured in this collage of high school friends from the class of 1877 are, from left to right, Etta Woods (in two pictures), Amanda Whetstone, and Tillie Severn.

These members of the class of 1876 are, clockwise from upper left, Ella Hurd (Burroughs), Amanda Whetstone, Dr. Arthur Jones, Ella Haughney (O'Donnell), Clara Yoder (Stine), and Michael P. Groody.

Elijah Bull was the first superintendent of the Mahanoy City public school system, from 1865 to 1868.

Channing Stebbins was the second superintendent of the Mahanoy City public school system. He served as superintendent from 1868 to 1869.

William Nelson Ehrhardt was the Mahanoy City High School principal from 1895 to 1896. Ehrhardt also served as the seventh superintendent of the Mahanoy City public school system for 18 years, from 1896 to 1914.

James Brunner was the first Mahanoy City high school principal, from 1864 to 1865. His bride, Anna K. Wilson, was a Mahanoy City primary school teacher from 1863 to 1865. They were married in 1866.

These three Mahanoy City public school teachers are also cousins. They taught in the 1870s. Shown, from left to right, are Mary Whetstone, Amanda Whetstone, and Hannah Whetstone.

These three Mahanoy City grammar school teachers in the 1890s are, from left to right, Minnie Dipper, Ella Haughney, and Hattie Wagner.

The Richardson sisters were all schoolteachers through the years in the Mahanoy City public school system. Shown, from left to right, are Ella, who taught in the 1960s; Mary (died 1867), who taught in the 1960s; Maggie, who taught in the 1970s; and Fannie, who taught in the 1980s.

"The Teachers' Corps" in 1878 poses in front of the old Pine Street school building in Mahanoy City.

Mary J. McHugh, at the age of 13 years old, was the youngest teacher in the Mahanoy City public school system. She taught from the 1860s to the 1880s.

John Linlon, a teacher for 41 years in the Mahanoy City public school system, was in the profession longer than any other teacher was in the school system.

This is a picture of Orlando C. Tiffany, the first grammar school teacher in Mahanoy City. He taught from 1866 to 1878 in the Spruce Street building.

Four

INDUSTRIES

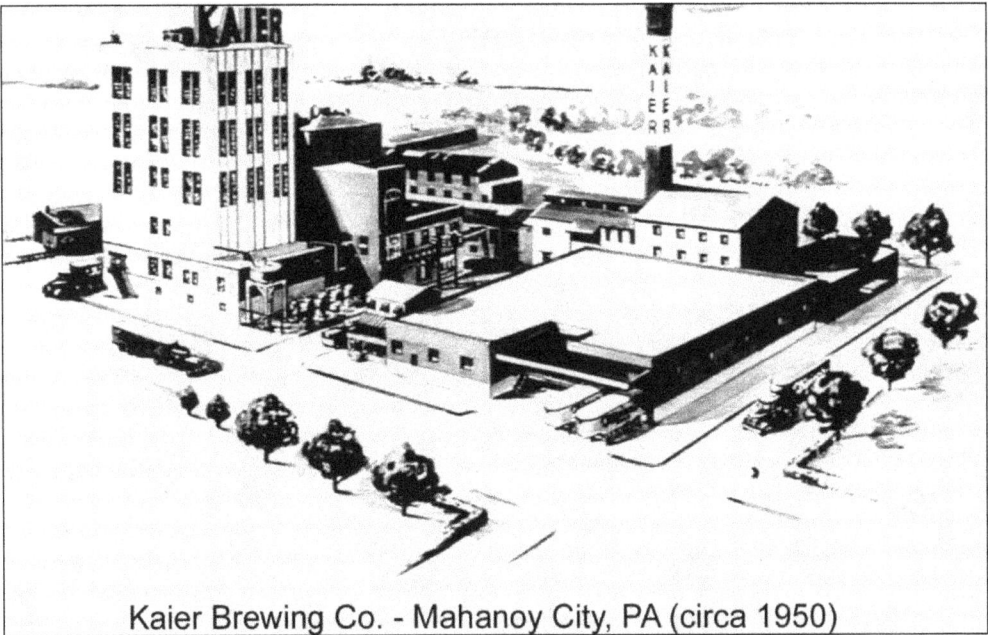

Kaier Brewing Co. - Mahanoy City, PA (circa 1950)

The Kaier Brewery was erected in 1883 on North Main Street and Commercial Alley. By 1912, it was producing 100,000 barrels of beer per year. The state-of-the-art facility had its own blacksmith, tinsmith, plumbing, carpenter, and cooperage shops, as well as the largest individual ice plant in the vicinity.

Annual Banquet to Employees, by Mrs. Chas. D. Kaier

This 1911 photograph shows the annual employee banquet, hosted by Margaret Kaier, president of the Kaier Brewery. Kaier (center), who was also celebrating her 72nd birthday, is sitting next to her son Charles F. Kaier. Her daughters, also seated at the table, are Josephine (wife of Michael Haughney), Margaret (wife of John B. Lieberman), Mary "Mame" (wife of

Lloyd W. Fahler), Cresentia (wife of Richard Kirby), and Amelia (wife of Henry Schreyer). The Kaiers had four other children: Bridget, Anna, and Troian Anselm, who all died at a very young age; and Ella (wife of John B. Lieberman), who died in 1895.

Just as Budweiser is noted today for its Clydesdale team, so was the Kaier Brewery of Mahanoy City once noted for its six-horse team. This 1912 photograph shows the team in front of the Kaier House Hotel, just down Main Street from the brewery, hitched to a wagon laden with wooden barrels of amber fluid. In the background, at the north end of Main Street, is the Lehigh Valley Depot.

The Mahanoy City Light, Heat and Power Company was organized in 1887 by E. S. Silliman, Andrew Comery, and W. L. Yoder. In that same year, 1,084 out of 1,139 citizens voted for the electrification of the town, and a contract was issued for the erection of poles and wires. Pictured on Vine Street, the cement block edifice remains at its original location.

The first newspaper in Mahanoy City, the *Mahanoy Gazette*, was established in 1865. It changed names and owners several times until, in 1909, it was purchased by James H. Kirchner, pictured here at his desk at the newspaper. Under Kirchner's leadership, the daily paper merged with the *Daily American* and became known as the *American Tribune*. In 1919, another merger with the *Mahanoy Record* changed the name to the *Record-American*. The *Record-American* was operated by Kirchner and his heirs under the same name for more than 50 years until it merged with the *Shenandoah Evening Herald* in 1969. (Courtesy of James Owens.)

Located at 29–31 West Pine Street, this vacant Record-American building was the last remnant of a century of daily newspaper publications in Mahanoy City. The structure was demolished in March 2004 as part of a borough-sponsored redevelopment project. The *Record-American* came into existence in 1919, when James H. Kirchner effected a consolidation of three earlier Mahanoy papers: the *Record* (dating from 1871), the *Tribune* (1881), and the *American* (1890). Kirchner's heirs wrote finis to the business by selling it to the *Shenandoah Evening Herald* in April 1969. (Courtesy of Bill O'Brien.)

Saule, "the sun," was founded in 1888 by Dominick Boczkowski in Mahanoy City. It was the first Lithuanian newspaper in the United States. It was mailed nationally until it went out of business in 1969. From its beginning, it was located in a wood-frame building at the corner of West South and A Streets. Frank Boczkowski (left) became the editor when his father died in 1909. The advertisement below appeared in the 50th-anniversary souvenir booklet of 1913.

1865—SEMI-CENTENNIAL OF MAHANOY CITY—1915

Established 1888   The Oldest Lithuanian Paper in the World

THE SEMI-WEEKLY

SAULE

THE SUN.

Has a Larger Circulation than any other Lithuanian Paper.   Brings the Best Results to Advertisers.
Rates on Application

PUBLISHED EVERY TUESDAY AND FRIDAY

Subscription $2.50

Representing the Interest of Over 500,000 Lithuanians Residing in the United States

PUBLISHED BY

W. D. BOCZKOWSKI-CO.

520-522 W. SOUTH AL.   MAHANOY CITY, PA.

The North Mahanoy colliery opened in 1858, when Edward and Samuel Silliman drove a drift into the hillside near Bowman's Patch, a half-mile north of the borough. The first coal shipment, in 1860, totaled 540 tons. In 1863, the colliery was the first to ship coal through the Mahanoy Tunnel. When fire destroyed the breaker in 1869, the colliery was sold to Rommel, Hill & Harris, who also owned the nearby Mahanoy City colliery, also known as "Hill's Colliery." A new breaker (above) opened in 1870, and the colliery was acquired in 1873 by the Philadelphia & Reading Coal and Iron Company. In 1931, the breaker was shut down after the the new central breaker started at St. Nicholas.

Silliman's Washery opened in 1869 as an addition to the North Mahanoy colliery. It was situated on the hillside, just north of the other colliery structures.

79

Hill's Colliery was started in 1860 by Hill and Harris, who drove a drift into the mammoth vein. The first shipment of coal, in 1862, was 12,240 tons. A new double breaker with a capacity of 600 tons daily was put into service in 1870. In 1873, the Philadelphia & Reading Coal and Iron Company purchased the colliery and boosted shipments to 127,000 tons a year. The breaker was abandoned in 1931, when the St. Nicholas central breaker opened, and was torn down in 1936. All Mahanoy colliery mining ceased in 1953.

A bond between a driver boy and his mine mule is evident in this scene at one of the Mahanoy district collieries. Any such attempt to recline on the back of the mule at rest was an act that could have been hazardous to the health of a lad with whom the four-legged miner was not adequately acquainted.

At an age when today's boys would be in a third-grade classroom, these youngsters of anthracite's pioneer era spent nine hours a day, six days a week picking slate from the constant stream of coal flowing down chutes in the breaker. They sat on crude wooden perches, bent over the chutes, fingertips rubbed painfully raw, lungs filled with the black dust everywhere around them. If a piece of slate should slip by, the boy received a prod from a stick wielded by the ever-present old chute boss watching from behind. The pay was 5¢ an hour.

John J. Curtis (center) was born in 1863 and lost his eyesight as a result of an explosion in the Morea mine in 1888. After Curtis became blind, Joseph Gallagher of Lansford composed a ballad for him, and broadsides were printed for him by the *Lansford Record*. Curtis roamed the country reciting or singing the ballad in order to make a living, as there was no worker compensation in those days. He died in 1932 on a farm in Barnesville, while living with his brothers. Pictured with him are, from left to right, the following: (seated) brothers James (a Spanish-American War veteran) and Joseph Curtis; (standing) brother Patrick Curtis and brother-in-law William Selgrath Sr.

In 1919, the old Vulcan and Buck Mountain collieries, built by the Mill Creek Coal Company in the 1860s, were passed to the Lehigh Valley Coal Company after a 50-year lease ended. A new division of the Lehigh Valley was formed, with headquarters in Mahanoy City under superintendent William Underwood of Wilkes-Barre. The breaker was constructed from steel, located about one-quarter mile west of the Vulcan patch. At the same time, 20 double homes were built northwest of the breaker and named the Underwood Patch after the first superintendent.

Mine boss Tom Ward gives instruction to Owen O'Neil. Note the whale oil lamp used in the early days of mining. (Courtesy of Ray Eichman.)

New Boston Colliery,
Mahanoy City, Pa.

The Delano family from Boston, Massachusetts, owned tracts of land near Delano and New Boston and formed the New Boston Coal Mining Company. The first mine drift was opened in 1864, and the first breaker was built 1865. The property was sold in 1871 to the Broad Mountain and Lehigh Company and was reorganized in 1873 as the Middle Lehigh Company. The breaker burned on October 12, 1893, and was rebuilt in 1904.

Gilberton Water Shaft : 1100 ft. deep ;
Hoisting Cap., 384,000 Gal. per hour

This 1,000-foot-deep shaft at the sharp curve entering the east end of Gilberton Borough was used to hoist water from the mine. The shaft worked around the clock, removing 384,000 gallons per hour by means of huge tanks attached to the hoisting engine cables. The advent of powerful steam pumps replaced the tank system in the late 1800s, and the shaft was used for regular mining purposes. Today, water from the shaft is used by the cogeneration plant atop Broad Mountain, east of Frackville.

The Morea Supply Company was a general store attached to the Morea Colliery. The village and colliery took its name from Morea Lea, the daughter of the store manager.

The old St. Nicholas breaker received its name in 1861 because the initial run of coal took place on Christmas Day. The mine that supplied the breaker with raw coal was opened in 1858 by Henry Geist, who drove a drift into the hillside. Henry L. Cake joined Geist as a partner in 1861, and he named the operation. The breaker was torn down in 1928 to make way for the new central plant, which was constructed a short distance to the north.

Tunnel Ridge Colliery was opened in 1862 by George W. Cole at the base of Broad Mountain, where the Mahanoy Area High School football stadium now stands. A year later, the first coal (28,000 tons) was shipped to market. In 1879, the colliery was acquired by the Philadelphia & Reading Coal and Iron Company, which erected a new breaker (pictured) that remained in service until the St. Nicholas central breaker opened in 1931.

It was payday at Tunnel Ridge Colliery when this photograph was taken in 1905. Mineworkers usually received their pay twice monthly. The presence of women and men in Sunday attire indicates that some sort of celebration was in the offing—perhaps a picnic excursion by train to Lakeside Park.

Perched on a huge steel bucket, with several hundred feet of open shaft beneath them, are members of the excavation crew engaged in sinking the vertical mine opening at Maple Hill Colliery in the late 1890s. The wet rain slickers worn by some of the laborers illustrates the added difficulty confronting them from a constant flow of water that leaked from subterranean crevices in the rock strata down along the shaft walls. The photograph below shows an example of a drift mine, one that tunnels horizontally into the seam of coal. (Courtesy of Ray Eichman.)

The old railway motorcar was a quick and handy way for officials to conduct an inspection of trackage and other facilities. This scene is on the Lehigh Valley division, encompassing the Delano and Hazleton districts. It appears the car is headed the wrong way on a one-way double track.

This powerful Lehigh Valley machine is identified as an American ditcher, which kept drainage channels open alongside the tracks. In a pinch, it might also be adapted for other heavy tasks. The smokestack on the roof of the cab indicates it was steam powered.

Springdale Shaft, as it appears today at Bowman's Patch, has not changed much since it first opened 140 years ago. It is the last mining structure of its type in the Mahanoy Valley, where mine shafts once abounded. Springdale Shaft was opened by the Lentz Lilly Company on ground leased from the Delano Land Company. After operating for 30 years, it was abandoned in 1897 and began to fill with water, which posed a danger to adjacent mines. As a precaution, the Philadelphia & Reading Coal and Iron Company assumed pumping operations at the shaft, which reopened in 1914 and remained active on a limited basis until the 1940s. The photograph below shows the interior of the engine house hoisting mechanism.

A STORE GROUP IN 1910

Delano's hub of daily activity during the latter 1800s and early 1900s was the general store–post office, pictured here in 1910. It was open for business daily (except the Fourth of July and Christmas) from 6:00 a.m. to 9:00 p.m., and customers could have their purchases delivered via the wagons on the left. The store was privately owned; the most noted proprietor was Alonzo Blakeslee (1870s–1898), who was superintendent of the Lehigh Valley Railroad's Mahanoy division. Among those pictured are store manager Joseph Depew (front right) and postmaster George Hoffman (front, fourth from the right).

THE LOKIE ENGINE L.V. COAL CO.

Some of the earliest versions of a mine lokie (a small working locomotive) and coal cars are depicted in this scene at an unidentified Lehigh Valley Coal Company colliery.

RESIDENCE OF R. R. LEE.

— MANUFACTURERS OF —
STEAM ENGINES, STEAM PUMPS,
ROLLING MILL, FURNACE AND
MINING MACHINERY.   R. R. LEE.

GRANT IRON WORKS
LEE & WREN

MAHANOY

The Grant Iron Works, located just west of Mahanoy City, was a major developer of specialized mining machinery for collieries throughout the Mahanoy region and beyond from the 1860s to the early 1900s. The main man behind this vital industry was Thomas Wren, who conducted a similar enterprise in Pottsville for 14 years before expanding to Mahanoy in 1864. His brother

George Wren and Ralph Lee, who helped run the Pottsville plant, joined the Mahanoy site as supervisors. The ironworks was phased out around the time of World War I. The property was taken over in 1920 by L. A. Lutz, who turned it into a lumber business, which functioned through the 1950s.

Standing at the north end of Mahanoy City's Main Street, this 19th-century structure housed the office of the Philadelphia & Reading Coal and Iron Company land agent. The land agent's job was to make monthly rounds to collect rent from occupants of the firm's many mine patch tenant houses and from those leasing coal lands. The office was closed in 1957, when the bankrupt company divested its tenant dwellings.

Five

PATCHES, NEIGHBORHOODS, AND VILLAGES

This crumbling structure in the western corner of Mahanoy Township is a relic of the turbulent era of murder and mayhem that marked much of the 19th century in the anthracite region of northeastern Pennsylvania. The two decades of violence, referred to as "the Molly Maguire Reign of Terror," were especially prevalent in the southern coal fields, where the Mahanoy area is situated. Blame for practically all mining-related crimes was directed at a small number of Irish immigrants in a secret society known as the Molly Maguires. Their motives were purported to be reprisals against mine bosses who practiced discrimination and oppression in the workplace. The violence occurred mostly during the 1860s and 1870s and culminated with a retaliatory attack upon suspected "Mollies," who were among 10 people residing in this house, in Wiggans Patch. At 3:00 a.m. on December 10, 1875, a band of masked vigilantes burst into the dwelling while the occupants slept. Shots rang out, and when the intruders fled the scene two people lay dead, Ellen McAllister and her brother Charles O'Donnell. A third victim was added when it was learned that McAllister was pregnant with her second child. No one was ever tried for the slayings, which became known as the Wiggans Patch Massacre; however, it was the end for the Molly Maguires. Within three years, 20 alleged Mollies were hanged at various anthracite region prisons, including 10 who went to the gallows in one day, Thursday, June 21, 1877, in Pottsville and Mauch Chunk (now known as Jim Thorpe). This era will be memorialized with Molly Maguire Park, to be constructed in the near future at Center and Catawissa Streets in Mahanoy City.

1850 — 1860

THE OLD PATCHES

OF MAHANOY TOWNSHIP

	FORMED
RUSH TWP.	1811
MAHANOY TWP.	1849
MAHANOY CITY	1863
RYAN	1866
WEST. MAH. TWP.	1874

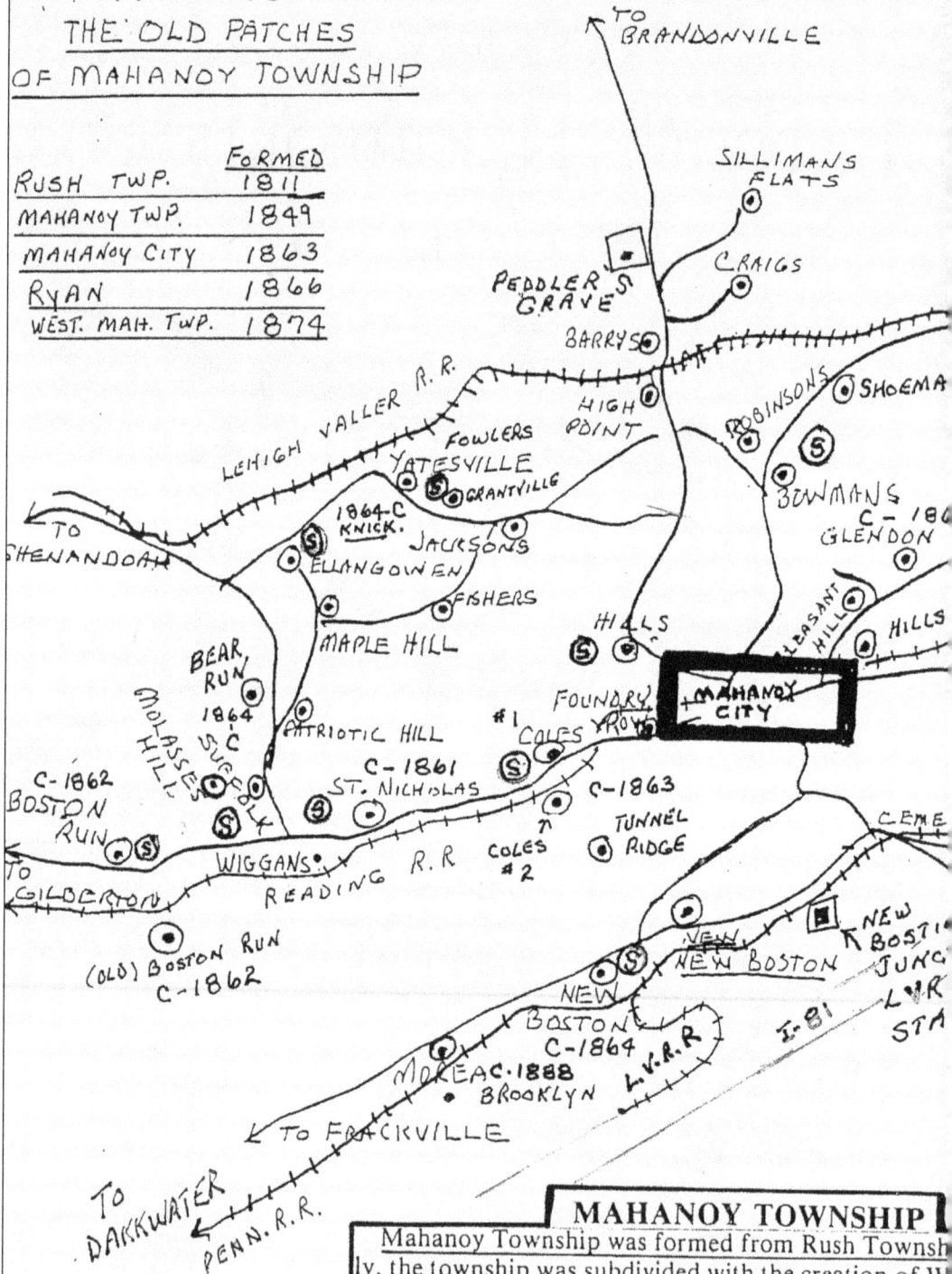

TO BRANDONVILLE

SILLIMANS FLATS

PEDDLER'S GRAVE

CRAIGS

BARRYS

HIGH POINT

ROBINSONS

SHOEMA

LEHIGH VALLEY R.R.

FOWLERS

YATESVILLE

GRANTVILLE

BEWMANS
C — 18

GLENDON

1864-C KNICK.

JACKSONS

TO SHENANDOAH

ELLANGOWEN

FISHERS

MAPLE HILL

HILLS

PLEASANT HILL

HILLS

BEAR RUN 1864 C

MOLASSES HILL

SUFFOLK

PATRIOTIC HILL

FOUNDRY ROW

MAHANOY CITY

C — 1862

BOSTON RUN

C — 1861

ST. NICHOLAS

#1 COLES ROW

C — 1863

TUNNEL RIDGE

CEME

TO GILBERTON

WIGGANS

READING R.R.

COLES #2

TO FRACKVILLE

(OLD) BOSTON RUN C — 1862

NEW

NEW BOSTON

NEW BOSTO JUNG

LVR STA

I-81

NEW BOSTON C — 1864

MOREA C. 1888

BROOKLYN

LV.R.R.

TO DARKWATER

PENN. R.R.

FRANK A SELGRATH — 1999

MAHANOY TOWNSHIP

Mahanoy Township was formed from Rush Towns
ly, the township was subdivided with the creation of W
and the boroughs of Mahanoy City, Shenandoah an

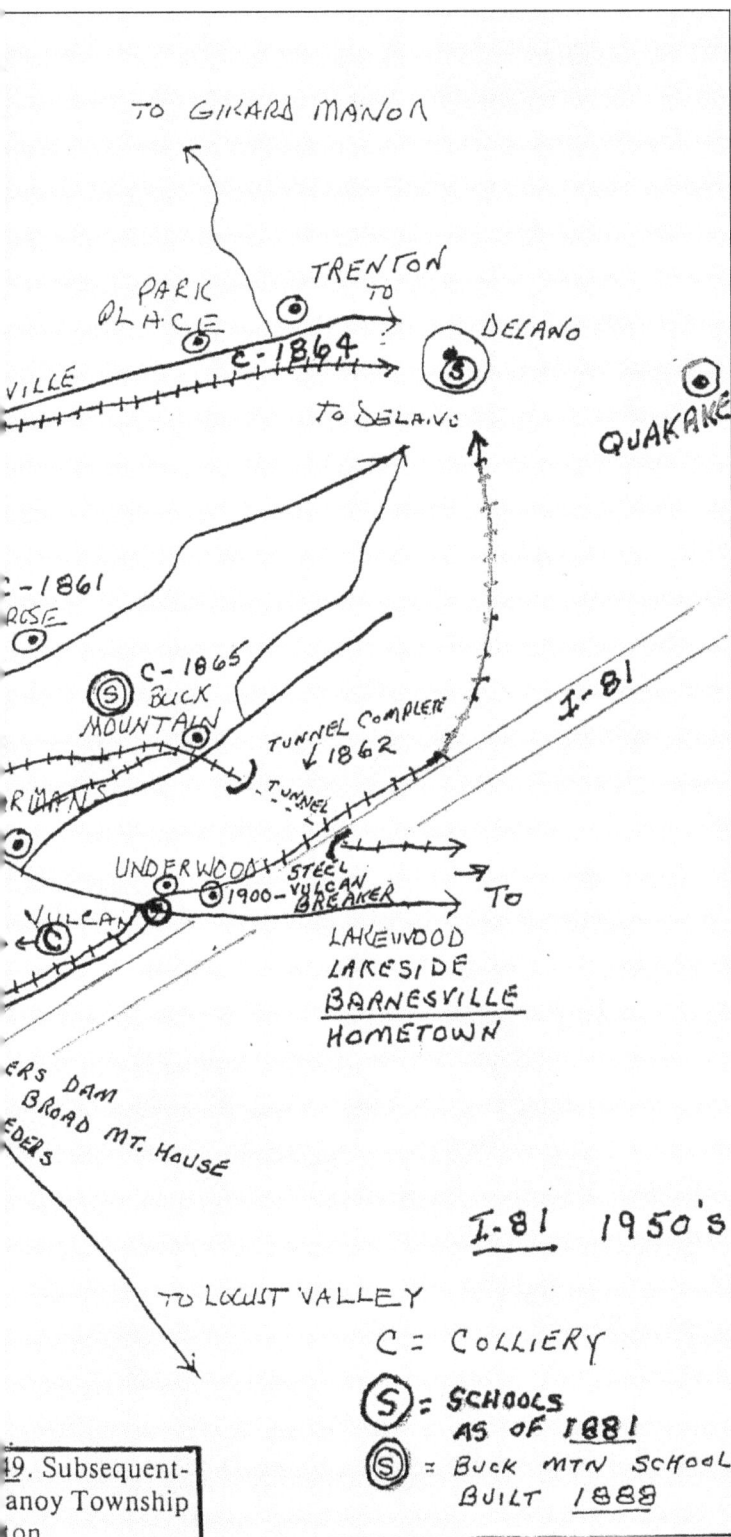

TO GIRARD MANOR

PARK PLACE

TRENTON
TO

...VILLE

DELANO

C - 1864

TO DELANO

QUAKAKE

C - 1861
ROSE

C - 1865
BUCK MOUNTAIN

TUNNEL COMPLEX
1862

I-81

...RMANS

TUNNEL

UNDERWOOD
STEEL
1900 - VULCAN BREAKER

TO

VULCAN

LAKEWOOD
LAKESIDE
BARNESVILLE
HOMETOWN

...ERS DAM
BROAD MT. HOUSE
...DERS

I-81   1950's

TO LOCUST VALLEY

C = COLLIERY

(S) = SCHOOLS AS OF 1881

(S) = BUCK MTN SCHOOL BUILT 1889

...9. Subsequent-
...anoy Township
...on

Mahanoy Township is the mine patch capital of the world. In the 200-year history of anthracite mining, no other municipality has contained as many of these unique coal-related villages, 35 in all. Although most are now a small fraction of the size they were when coal was booming, 22 are still in existence. The term "mine patch" is used only in the anthracite region and, most especially, in the southern coal fields in the Mahanoy area. It describes a cluster of simple dwellings erected by mining firms to house employees. Monthly rental fees were usually deducted from the tenants' paychecks. These dwellings were not considered part of a colliery but were "patched" to a colliery and included in a company's overall site. The patch usually took the name of its colliery, such as Hill's Patch at Hill's Colliery. Other had geographical connotations, such as Boston Run. Some were named in honor of significant dates, such as St. Nicholas's Patch. Today, coal companies own none of the patches. As the coal industry waned, the dwellings were put up for sale to the tenants, but the civilization of patch folk they fostered remains very much an integral part of the regional scene.

95

Old Boston Run is probably the oldest patch in Mahanoy Township. Births have been documented there as early as 1849, the year Mahanoy Township was formed. Patrick and Mary (Reid) Brown were married in Pottsville in 1848. They settled shortly afterward in Boston Run, where their first two children were born: Mary on October 15, 1849, and Margaret on November 21, 1851.

George Cole, whose company founded Tunnel Ridge Colliery, erected these homes to provide housing for his workers in Cole's Patch. Several similar homes were built a short distance to the east and were known as Cole's No. 2. Cole's Patch was the site of the first township high school, from 1900 to 1916.

This is one of the last six homes remaining in the Ellengowen Patch, which dates from c. 1860 and once numbered more than 60 dwellings. The site originally was known as Maple Dale, and the first two colliery owners were named Fisher and Lanigan, whose names were attached to the patch. In 1870, the site was acquired by the Philadelphia & Reading Coal and Iron Company, whose chief, Franklin B. Gowen, named the area after his sister Ellen. The dwelling above was reserved for the top boss at the colliery.

Herman Gilfert (left) was 20 years old when he came from Tamaqua to settle in Ellengowen in 1873. Until his demise in 1937, he worked as a lokie runner and colliery maintenance mechanic. He is shown with his siblings at a 1910 gathering in Coaldale. He was the only one of the clan to settle in the Mahanoy area, where some of his current descendants include a grandson, Luther Holt of Mahanoy City, whose electronic ingenuity played a key role in creating the Service Electric Cable TV & Communications system, and a great-grandson, David Linkchorst, the legendary Mahanoy athlete-coach of Park Crest.

Hill's Patch was also known as Hill's Terrace. This village is one of the oldest in Mahanoy Township, dating from the late 1850s. The age is reflected in the small tenant houses pictured here. The patch took its name from Hill's Colliery, which later became Mahanoy City Colliery. The road in front of the homes was the old Catawissa Turnpike, built in the mid-1700s to connect the Schuylkill River near Reading to the Susquehanna River near Bloomsburg.

Among the early settlers in Jackson's Patch was the Lawrence Keating family, two members of whom are pictured here. The clan later resided in Mahanoy City, Gilberton, and Mahanoy Plane (the Corktown section). Jackson's Patch was founded in the 1860s and named after Henry Jackson, an official of the nearby McNeal Colliery operations. Jackson also operated a store in Mahanoy City at 137–139 West Centre Street. Another official of the McNeal Colliery was Patrick Barry, who directed construction of the historic Mahanoy Tunnel. He owned a store at 17–19 West Centre Street, and Barry's Patch was named after him. Both villages were wiped out by strip mining in the 1960s.

Dating from 1895, the Maple Hill Patch was the last to be built in Mahanoy Township. This photograph illustrates one of the front row dwellings, which were reserved for colliery bosses and their families.

Shanty Hill Patch was built in the 1860s. In 1918, during a flag-raising ceremony, the orator, attorney M. M. Burke of Shenandoah, lauded the villagers for their patriotism and the name was changed to Patriotic Hill Patch. This house is the birthplace of John Walsonavich, founder of the world's first cable television system, Service Electric Cable TV & Communications, in 1947.

St. Nicholas's Patch ceased to be a residential site in December 2003, when the last tenanted house (pictured) was vacated, thus ending a 137-year history. In the background is the huge colliery culm bank. This village originally was known as Cakes Patch, after a coal firm official.

Shown is what remains of an outdoor oven in Suffolk Patch that housewives used for baking.

This is a recent picture of one of the original homes built in the 1860s in Bowman's Patch. It is located in Mahanoy Township, northeast of Mahanoy City along the Park Place-Delano Road near the former Bowman's Colliery. The colliery and patch were named after the Bowman brothers—David Sr., Peter, Henry, and Jonas—who operated the colliery starting in 1862. Prior to 1880, a school was built in Bowman's Patch that was used by students from nearby patches.

This mine patch at Yatesville was built in the early 1860s. The village originally was known as Fowler's, in honor of Malachi P. Fowler. Fowler was a coal prospector who opened the first mine there, along with his partner, Henry Kuhn. Fowler and Kuhn shipped their first coal on November 23, 1864. The mine was sold in 1865 to a New York City firm, the Knickerbocker Coal Company, whose president was Isaac Hayes, the famed Arctic explorer. A captain named Yates was appointed superintendent of the colliery, and the site took on his name. The Philadelphia & Reading Coal and Iron Company assumed control in 1873 and ran the colliery until it closed in 1954.

Jennie (Jane) Coll Curtis, wife of Joseph Curtis, was a daughter of one of the earliest Buck Mountain Patch families. The Coll and Curtis families were lifelong residents of that patch. Jennie and Joseph Curtis had three daughters: Margaret Curtis, Mary (Curtis) Frey, and Catherine (Curtis) Wronski. (Courtesy of Frank Selgrath.)

This house is located on an 18-acre farm east of Barnesville, along the railroad. According to an 1870 deed, it was owned by John S. Boyer and sold to Ruben Stahler, who later sold it to Samuel Yost in 1874. The property was sold numerous times in later years and was purchased by William Selgrath and James Curtis in 1920 from Raymond and Bessie Boyer.

In the early 1860s, the Lehigh Valley Railroad was extended west from Delano. The Park Place Colliery was built *c.* 1864 by Lentz, Lily, and Company. A company store was built near the first three houses close to the railroad, which were occupied by the Swartz, Clarkson, and Butler families. As the village expanded, a school and more houses for colliery employees were built nearby. Many of these remain occupied today, after much remodeling by the owners. (Information from *The History of Park Place*, researched by Allison Moucheron and Tabitha Bumbulsky for a school project in 1998.)

Eisenhuth Reservoir Lodge is located on Broad Mountain in Ryan Township, south of Morea and Route 181. The dam was ordered to be built in 1871 to supply water for residents of St. Clair, Pottsville, Palo Alto, and Port Carbon. In later years, this lodge and surrounding cabins were built as a resort for Reading Railroad officials. At the same time, a home was built for a year-round caretaker and his family. The caretaker's children attended the nearest school, located at Morea in Mahanoy Township. The reservoir is currently owned by the Schuylkill County Water Authority, and the caretaker now resides in this lodge.

Robinson's Patch was named for J. O. Robinson, manager of Robinson's Colliery (old Primose Mine, 1861). He was a brother-in-law of the colliery owner and former owner of a store at 33 East Centre Street in Mahanoy City. A school and more houses were built later. The school was still used in the 1930s, and 15 houses existed at one time, only 1 of which remains.

Shoemaker's Patch is located about one mile north of Mahanoy City along the road to Park Place, near the former Lehigh Valley Railroad. Houses were built for employees of the West Lehigh Colliery in the late 1860s.

New Boston is located on the Vulcan-Frackville highway near the intersection of the road leading to Mahanoy City. Houses were built c. 1864 on a New Boston Land Company tract of land. At the same time, the newly formed Mill Creek Coal Company proved that there were coal veins in the area worth mining. A railroad was built to connect with Delano, and a coal breaker was built in 1868. Prior to 1875, a school was built, as was done in many of the patches. Franklin Delano Roosevelt visited the house above when he was a young boy.

They have been working on the railroad. With a shortage of males during the World War I draft, area railroads turned to women and children to perform track maintenance. This corps is pictured on the Reading line at the Wiggans train stop shed.

Located on the other side of Broad Mountain from Mahanoy City is the idyllic Locust Valley, in Ryan Township. Spared the ravages of coal mining, it was primarily a farming community. The Mountain View Hotel (above) operated in the heart of the valley for many years and was formerly known as Wards Hotel. The structure below is situated approximately at the spot where the valley's first settler, David Dreshe, built his home in 1790.

Bridge Street, Mahanoy Plane Pa.

The town of Mahanoy Plane, in Gilberton Borough, was named for the inclined plane that carried coal from the Mahanoy Valley up Broad Mountain to Frackville. The plane can be seen in the background of the photograph above. The large building on the left of the photograph below is the Union House Hotel, built in 1863.

Main Street, Mahanoy Plane Pa.

Wiggans Patch was named in honor of George Wiggan, owner of the nearby Bear Run Colliery. This village originally included the adjoining settlements of Molasses Hill and part of the patch currently designated as Boston Run. Wiggans Patch had its own schoolhouse until the mid-1930s.

Six

LEISURE AND CIVIC GROUPS

Mahoney City, Pa.   7000 Humane S. F. Co. No. 1

The need for an organized fire company was felt early in the history of Mahanoy City. In 1867, a group of the borough's most prominent citizens joined to form the Humane Fire Company No. 1. The company had one piece of equipment, a hand-drawn hose carriage, shown in front of the firehouse.

In 1893, a group of 19 German men organized the third volunteer fire company in Mahanoy City, under the charter name of the German American Hose Company. In 1919, its name was changed to the Good American Hose Company, but the majority of its members continued to

be of German descent. For many years, the "Dutchies" (from the German "Deutsche") operated a coal and ice business that, along with membership dues, maintained fine meeting quarters and a hose house. (Courtesy of the Good American Hose Company.)

Fred Klitsch of East Mahanoy Avenue is pictured on the right in his Civil War uniform. Klitsch was one of the founding members of the German American Hose Company. Organized in 1893, the company kept its minutes in the German language. Prompted by America's anti-German sentiment during World War I, the company changed its name in 1919 to the Good American Hose Company, but its affiliation with individuals of German descent lasted well into the 20th century.

The Citizen's Cornet Band was established in 1868, with Jacob Britz as the band leader. It was popular at the time for fraternal organizations to organize bands for entertainment and fellowship. The Lithuanian and German organizations also had bands.

Shortly after a fire, during which volunteers needed to borrow a ladder from a painter to reach the upper story, the Washington Hook and Ladder Company was organized, and a charter for 100 members was drawn. This horse-drawn equipment, c. 1886, was purchased by the fire company, located in the Second Ward of Mahanoy City.

The Citizen's Steam Fire Company No. 2 was granted a charter in 1873. Milton Bowman was instrumental in its organization in 1870. The fire company purchased a steam fire engine in 1875 and named it Lady Jane Smith, in honor of the largest donor, Jane Smith. The first equipment was pulled by hand until horses took over from 1877 to 1917, when a motor-pulled engine was purchased.

Organized in 1900, the Knights of Columbus Council No. 549 erected this fine building in 1906 at 17–19 West Mahanoy Avenue to further promote its social and benevolent activities. The second floor was a large ballroom, where the Knights held many dances. A split entrance door and gaslight fixtures are still present. A bowling alley in the basement, where the Boy Scouts also met, is no longer there. In 1942, the library board of trustees purchased the Knights of Columbus building for use as the public library. The building still serves that function and looks much as it did in 1906.

The Patriotic Order of the Sons of America was one of the most prominent organizations in Mahanoy City at the turn of the 20th century. The group's large brick three-story building, erected in the 1890s, still stands at Second and Pine Streets. The lower two floors were built for tenants, and the third floor was used as a meeting hall.

To reach Lakeside Park from Mahanoy City and the surrounding villages, people boarded the train at the depot on North Main and Railroad Streets and rode 20 minutes to the East Mahanoy Junction at Lakeside (pictured), which was located across Route 54 from the park entrance. The train depot still exists and has been converted to a single-family dwelling.

Walk from Lake to Hotel, Lakeside Park, East Mahonoy Junction, Pa.

Lakeside Park is pictured in this early postcard view, which looks south from the lake and pavilion area. Sometimes called "Lover's Lane," this tree-lined walk extended from the hotel and train depot across the highway to the lake, where couples took canoe rides and enjoyed picnic lunches.

Lakeside Park was the scene of many outings for civic groups, businesses, and families. Pictured at a picnic in the park are James Kirschner, owner of the *Record-American* newspaper, and his dog. In the left background is an antique lindy loop ride, and in the right background, a wooden roller coaster. The roller coaster was later blown down in a hurricane.

This press-release photograph is an original of Victor Schertzinger, a Hollywood director, composer, and conductor. Schertzinger was born in Mahanoy City in 1890 and was raised in his family's jewelry store on Centre Street. At age 10, he played with the John Philip Sousa Band. He went on to a career in the movies, in which he won an Academy Award for composing the score for *One Night of Love*.

EAST END PARK, SHOWING CHILDREN'S WADING POOL, MAHANOY CITY, PA.

The East End Park opened in 1905 and featured a swimming pool, bathhouse, and playground. On June 30, 1910, a tennis court and a basketball court were added. The park had swings, slides, a trapeze, a drum ride, a carousel, a picnic grove, and a World War I monument.

Bird's Eye View
Mahanoy City, Pa.

The West End Park, located in Mahanoy Township just west of the borough line, was the center of sports and athletic activity for more than a century. In the early 1900s, Lizzie Stride, a Mahanoy City native, played baseball in this stadium. She went on to play semiprofessional ball with the Keystone minor-league baseball team of Reading. In 1923, during an exhibition game, Babe Ruth hit several home runs from the stadium into the churchyard of the Assumption of the Blessed Virgin Mary Church.

117

These students, in a surgical dressing class, are nurses with the Mahanoy City chapter of the American Red Cross at the beginning of the 20th century.

These instructors in surgical dressing are also with the Mahanoy City chapter of the American Red Cross.

Mahanoy City Lodge No. 695 Benevolent and Protective Order of Elks was instituted in 1901 with a charter membership of 31. The first meeting place was in Knapp's Hall, which was soon outgrown. The lodge then secured rental space in the Kaier property on East Centre Street (right). In 1914, the lodge purchased an addition to its quarters, a lot on the west side, and began to build a beautiful structure (below), which was dedicated in 1916. Originally, the first floor was the Elks Theatre; the second floor included the grille, dining room, bowling alley, and billiard tables; and the third floor was a magnificent meeting room.

On a hot summer day in Locust Valley, a cool dip in the swimming pool at Ward's Hotel was a welcome treat.

Croquet was a popular leisure activity, especially of the wealthy. This formal photograph shows the Kaier girls, daughters of Charles D. and Margaret Kaier, with croquet mallets. (Courtesy of Joan Goodman.)

Seven

TRANSPORTATION

In the 19th century, transportation was limited to mostly horse-drawn buggies. People from Locust Valley could travel to and from Mahanoy City via Tom Ward's Tally-Ho, a mule-powered wagon. (Courtesy of Ray Eichman.)

This railroad engine, the Alexander Mitchell No. 341, was built in the Delano shops of the Lehigh Valley Railroad in 1877. This was the first engine built from scratch at the shop, and it was named after the first master mechanic there. The Delano shops built many more engines for the Lehigh Valley. (Courtesy of Francis Senglar.)

A Shop Group of Late 80's. Plate XXIX

Pictured in the late 1880s at the Delano car shop are, from left to right, the following: (first row) William Wagner, John Richardson, George Light, Curtis Kim, Edward Joslyn, John McHugh, Garrett Hartly, Jeffrey Haverstock, Frank Hassler, and John Boughner Sr.; (second row) Jacob Engel and John Bannan; (third row) James Jackson, Michael Carroll, Albert Bast, J. N. Swartz (later a doctor), Thomas Reddy, Harry Richelderfer, Patrick Neary, unidentified, Jacob Engel Sr., and John Boughner Jr.

Hotel and Pavilion, Lakeside Park, East Mahonoy, Junction, Pa.

The Lakeside Park Hotel and Pavilion, located adjacent to East Mahonoy Junction, was a popular attraction in the late 1800s and early 1900s. Many tourists arriving by train stayed at the hotel, and the pavilion was used for dancing and other indoor entertainment. In 1910, former Mahanoy City postmaster Frank F. Reed leased the Lakeside Hotel from the Lakeside Ice and Amusement Company and was proprietor for a couple of years.

P. & R. STATION, MAHANOY CITY, PA.

The first Philadelphia & Reading Railroad passenger freight station was probably built in the 1870s at the juncture of the spur track that ran on the east side of Kaier Brewery and connected to the Lehigh Valley Railroad. Later, the most recent passenger station was built to the west, nearer to North Main Street, and the original station was used strictly for freight. With the decline of the railroad industry in recent years, both stations have been demolished and all but one track have been removed. The existing track is currently owned and used by the Reading and Northern Railroad.

P. and R. Depot and Hotel, Lakeside Park, East Mahanoy Junction, Pa.

The Philadelphia & Reading Railroad depot is located at East Mahanoy Junction, near Lakeside Park. The exact date the depot was established has not been determined, but it was probably between 1850 and 1870. This depot was a hub of activity after the completion of the Mahanoy Tunnel, due to the transportation of vast amounts of anthracite coal from the Mahanoy Valley. It also played an important role in the development of the Lakeside Ice and Amusement Company as a tourist attraction.

HOOK & LADDER #1 ANSWERING "4 taps", MAHANOY CITY, Pa.

In the 19th century, firemen responded to alarms in horse-drawn fire apparatus. Here, the Washington Hook and Ladder Company drives down East Mahanoy Avenue in Mahanoy City, answering a "four taps" alarm.

This team of horses and the carriage were used in 1908 to transport guests of the Kaier Hotel. Hotel proprietor Frank F. Reed is pictured with his grandson Feger Reed sitting on his lap. He is also pictured in the first block of East Railroad Street with his favorite horse, Prince. (Courtesy of Frank Selgrath.)

In the early 1900s, open-air sightseeing buses were becoming popular for tourists. This picture, taken c. 1905 in Washington, D. C., shows a group from Mahanoy City. William Selgrath Sr. stands at the far left. Note the cobblestone street and solid rubber tires on the bus. (Courtesy of Frank Selgrath.)

The employee who operated the switching levers in this Reading Railroad junction tower at Mahanoy Plane routed trains through a maze of interlocking tracks. In addition to traffic moving on the main Tamaqua-Shamokin line, the interlocking tracks provided access to the Shenandoah branch via Lost Creek, the hoisting plane branch that led up the mountain to Frackville, or the car storage yards and repair shops in Mahanoy Plane.

The north end of the Mahanoy Tunnel, through the Vulcan Mountain, is seen here from Buck Mountain. The tunnel, which opened in 1862, allowed coal to be sent to major industrial sites quickly and efficiently. (Courtesy of Bill O'Brien.)

This huge fan at the southern portal of the Mahanoy Tunnel was used during the steam locomotive era to clear the tunnel of smoke and fumes. (Courtesy of Bill O'Brien.)

In 1889, the Schuylkill Traction Company built the first trolley road connecting Ashland, Girardville, and Gilberton to Centre Street in Mahanoy City. The trolley lines were abandoned in 1925, when busses became popular.

Looking north across the tracks, this view shows the Barnesville Railroad Station. The railroad and station were built under the patronage of the Little Schuylkill Railroad. In 1854, the East Mahanoy Railroad incorporated and leased this railroad, with the provision that it should connect the Mahanoy coal fields with the Little Schuylkill Navigation Company, five miles north of Tamaqua. The Reading Blue Mountain & Northern Railroad Company is the present owner.